Professionalism in the Office

Proven Techniques for Administrators, Secretaries, and Coordinators

Revised Edition

Marilyn Manning, Ph.D., CMC, CSP

A Fifty-Minute™ Series Book

This Fifty-Minute™ book is designed to be "read with a pencil." It is an excellent workbook for self-study as well as classroom learning. All material is copyright-protected and cannot be duplicated without permission from the publisher. *Therefore, be sure to order a copy for every training participant by contacting:*

Menlo Park, California

1-800-442-7477

CrispLearning.com

Professionalism in the Office

*Proven Techniques for Administrators,
Secretaries, and Coordinators*

Revised Edition (formerly *Professional Excellence for Secretaries*)

Marilyn Manning, Ph.D., CMC, CSP

CREDITS:
Senior Editor: **Debbie Woodbury**
Editor: **Eileen Cohen**
Production Editor: **Jill Zayszly**
Production Manager: **Judy Petry**
Design: **Nicole Phillips**
Production Artist: **Zach Hooker**
Cartoonist: **Ralph Mapson**

© 2001 Crisp Publications, Inc.
Printed in the United States of America by Von Hoffmann Graphics, Inc.

CrispLearning.com

01 02 03 04 10 9 8 7 6 5 4 3 2 1

Library of Congress Catalog Card Number 2001089533
Manning, Marilyn
Professionalism in the Office
ISBN 1-56052-606-8

Learning Objectives For:

PROFESSIONALISM IN THE OFFICE

The objectives for *Professionalism in the Office* are listed below. They have been developed to guide you, the reader, to the core issues covered in this book.

THE OBJECTIVES OF THIS BOOK ARE:

❑ 1) To help you position yourself as a professional

❑ 2) To discuss techniques for enhancing your professional image

❑ 3) To provide ideas for expanding skills and responsibilities

❑ 4) To describe practical ways to communicate for better results

❑ 5) To provide tips for building relationships and networks

ASSESSING YOUR PROGRESS

In addition to the learning objectives, Crisp Learning has developed an **assessment** that covers the fundamental information presented in this book. A 25-item, multiple-choice and true-false questionnaire allows the reader to evaluate his or her comprehension of the subject matter. To learn how to obtain a copy of this assessment, please call **1-800-442-7477** and ask to speak with a Customer Service Representative.

Assessments should not be used in any employee selection process.

Preface

Whether your job title reads Administrator, Secretary, Coordinator, or any number of other descriptions, you are a key member of your organization. In fact, you are your organization to many people. For example, when you are on the telephone or responding to a letter you speak for your organization.

It would be impossible to provide complete guidelines for all your varied duties in this brief book. Therefore, throughout, we will refer you to other self-studies in the Fifty-Minute Series™ that cover specific topics in more depth.

This self-study book will help you become even more promotable. When you make use of its principles and techniques, you will manage your job with less frustration, enjoy your job more, and enhance your professional value.

This edition has been revised to reflect the changing technologies and values in the workplace. Sections on emails, laptops, and LCD screens will help you use these tools to your advantage. As you deal with leadership, stress, and interruptions, this book will guide you in a politically correct and sensitive way.

Do you want to avoid last-minute assignments that make you feel frantic? Understand what your manager really means when he or she says three different things have top priority? Take your pencil and begin now. You have the control to make each day a step towards professional growth.

Marilyn Manning

Marilyn Manning, Ph.D.

About the Author

Marilyn Manning, Ph.D., is a certified management consultant, conflict mediator, and international speaker. She facilitates and coaches teams and leaders to solve difficult people problems and organizational challenges. Her interactive keynote speeches and workshop topics include Strategic Planning, Communications, Change and Conflict Management, Teambuilding, and Customer Service. Her clients include University of Chicago, Lucent, GE, Compaq, GTE, US Postal System, National Semiconductor, and Stanford Hospital.

For more information regarding programs by Dr. Marilyn Manning, contact her at 945 Mountain View Avenue, Mountain View CA 94040. Phone: 650-965-3663; email: M@MManning.com; website: www.MManning.com.

CONTENTS

Positioning Yourself
as a Professional

Developing a "Big Picture" Viewpoint

The difference between an office worker and a world-class professional administrator (or associate or administrative assistant) is a combination of personal confidence, polished skills, and a global, rather than task-oriented, approach to each day's possibilities.

As you work toward professional excellence, it is often helpful to model your behavior after someone you respect.

You will discover that highly successful employees have much in common. More than anything else, they share:

➤ A thorough knowledge of their organization's:

- goals, products, and services

- employees, clients (customers), executives

- history

- future possibilities

➤ The ability to perform each task so that the organization as a whole is best served

This means taking a global orientation. Those who concentrate on single tasks and never see "the bigger picture" are task-level workers.

Some examples of task-oriented and global-oriented behaviors are presented on the following page.

It's Your Choice

Your behavior at work conveys your level of professionalism. Review the two behavior styles below and make a conscious choice to transition from task-oriented to professional behaviors. By making this transition, you will naturally adapt a "big picture" viewpoint, or a global orientation of your organization.

Task-Oriented Behaviors

➤ Interrupts others whenever help is needed with individual tasks

➤ Keeps information the way it's always been, because it is easier

➤ Changes nothing unless instructed by a manager

➤ Answers each request individually, without noting patterns or trends

➤ Dreads messages from unhappy customers because of not knowing what to say

➤ Delays other department's requests "so they learn to do their own work"

➤ Once a project has begun, resists or refuses to alter its format or schedule

Add your own:

Waiting to be told rather than being proactive

Professional Behaviors

➤ Is sensitive to the "rhythm" of others and asks questions only at convenient times

➤ Updates and monitors electronic and hard-copy files, reflecting current needs of office personnel

➤ Notices revised contact information on incoming messages and makes appropriate changes immediately

➤ Notices when many inquiries ask similar questions and drafts a model response template to become more efficient

➤ Recognizes messages from unhappy customers as an opportunity to suggest improvements in company policies

➤ When another department requests assistance, helps (or finds help) as soon as possible

➤ When working on a project, is happy to insert last-minute changes, even if it means considerable additional work

Add your own:

Smile rather than grumble

Working with others, you have had the opportunity to observe contributions they have made and ways they have significantly helped an organization. List two that you recall.

1. Brande jumped into New organizational changes
2. Without Missing a step

Joe help ABC Website Committee setup Website

USE A GLOBAL ORIENTATION TO ANALYZE YOUR AREA

Use this worksheet to take a closer look at your organization. If you don't have all the information needed, ask a co-worker for help.

1. The type of work my area supports is:

   Administrative for Directors

2. Our customers or clients are:

   Pharm R&D Dept - Colleagues in Pharm Sci

3. Our main competitors are:

   Other Pharmaceutical Companies

4. As a team, are we doing better or worse than last year? Why?

   Keeping up with the Changes

5. Ways in which our business or organization has changed in the past several months:

   Departmental Changes, Supervisor Changes

6. Changes in our basic business that have caused changes in our procedures:

   Department Structure

7. Ways I feel we need to change to better support our customers or clients:

   Stay Current with New Software
   Be flexible and willing to learn

Being successful means seeing yourself as vital to your organization's progress. You can be the first to notice possibilities for change and improvement.

Your Attitude and Your Job

The "magic key" that opens your mind and heart to better job performance—and a better life—is *Your Attitude*.

A positive attitude helps you to:

➤ Consider your job as part of the larger pattern of your entire organization

➤ Visualize your potential when dealing with other employees, customers, and clients

➤ Understand how your attitude affects other people's attitudes and performance

Your skill in dealing with others is your most important asset. This book will show you how to approach every specific task or duty with a positive attitude.

What Is a Professional?

"Professional" refers to an attitude, not necessarily a job description. Professionals:

➤ Take their jobs seriously and view them as important to their career plans

➤ Analyze how the job could be better performed—even if it means making changes

➤ Understand how their jobs relate to the organization as a whole

➤ Feel confident about sharing ideas, goals, and enthusiasm with other people

Your professional attitude enhances all your other skills and enables you to use them more effectively.

YOUR ATTITUDE

To measure your attitude, complete the following exercise. Read each statement and then circle the appropriate number.

---
5 = Agree 1= Disagree

1.	I seek responsibility.	**(5)**	**4**	**3**	**2**	**1**
2.	Respect is important to me.	**(5)**	**4**	**3**	**2**	**1**
3.	I enjoy helping others.	**(5)**	**4**	**3**	**2**	**1**
4.	I want to know more about human behavior.	**(5)**	**4**	**3**	**2**	**1**
5.	I want to advance in my career.	**(5)**	**4**	**3**	**2**	**1**
6.	I am anxious to learn and master organizational skills.	**(5)**	**4**	**3**	**2**	**1**
7.	I like leadership and coordination situations.	**5**	**(4)**	**3**	**2**	**1**
8.	Working with a problem employee would be an interesting challenge.	**5**	**4**	**(3)**	**2**	**1**
9.	I intend to devote time to learn the latest technical skills and computer applications.	**(5)**	**4**	**3**	**2**	**1**
10.	I'm excited about learning to actualize my potential.	**(5)**	**4**	**3**	**2**	**1**

Total _47_

If you scored above 40, you have an excellent attitude toward becoming more professional. If you rated yourself between 25 and 40, it would appear you have a few reservations. A rating under 25 indicates you should rethink your attitude.

What Is an Office, Anyway?

There are offices everywhere in the world, from Australia to Zambia. And in every office, someone will be:

➤ On the computer

➤ Keeping office records and reports

➤ Screening calls and messages

➤ Distributing information

➤ Organizing systems and procedures

An office is not an end in itself. It is a "service" department to make the work of others more effective. An office exists to assist its workers, customers, and clients. Their needs are always changing. One of your challenges is to anticipate these needs and initiate appropriate changes.

Taking Action

People often claim they don't like "being in a rut," but then fight actual changes in their work methods. It is only natural to fear unknown consequences when you change your behavior. If this book gives you 20 ideas for managing your job differently, only you will know them. And you can decide, step-by-step, when and how you will put them into action.

Some people believe "changing their image" means not being true to who they really are. Professional growth comes when new ideas lead to new ways of seeing. If you look around and notice that people who are not expressing themselves professionally are not taken seriously, it makes sense to be aware of your own communication skills.

The "us vs. them" mentality among staff is very strong in some offices (particularly large ones). Some staff and "cliques" can feel loyalty to one another, rather than to the organization as a whole. This attitude stops professional growth, yet can seem comfortable and safe on a day-by-day basis.

Here are some tips that should help you feel comfortable about moving toward a more professional approach to work.

Making Changes Smoothly

➤ Change one thing at a time—slow and easy does it.

➤ Define your goal in simple, active, and positive words.

➤ Write your change goal and post it where you see it daily.

➤ If your change affects other people, tell them what you plan to do and why. Discuss your goal. If they have other ideas, listen. The discussion itself may lead to a better working relationship.

➤ A great deal of practice may be needed before a new behavior becomes natural.

Remember, you don't have to be perfect.

YOUR LEADERSHIP POTENTIAL

To help you set some career goals as you read this book, take a look at your leadership potential. Check (✔) all of these you can answer yes to.

- ☑ I look for positive challenges during periods of change.
- ☑ I am decisive, willing to take risks, and able to learn from mistakes.
- ☑ I regularly acknowledge others' accomplishments.
- ☑ I reflect the values I believe.
- ☑ I look for ways to share power.
- ☑ I delegate tasks with authority and decisiveness.
- ☐ I have written long-range plans and I'm committed to them.
- ☑ I create a motivational environment.
- ☑ I promote team effort and spirit.
- ☐ I regularly give honest, constructive feedback to my team.
- ☑ I make decisions in a timely manner.
- ☑ I stand up for what I believe.
- ☑ I expect to be treated with respect at all times.
- ☑ I respect the people who work with me.
- ☑ I clearly state my expectations.
- ☑ I evaluate what others have to say, but take full responsibility for the decisions I make.

CONTINUED

CONTINUED

Striving to answer "yes" on each of these is a worthy goal for any leader—especially for administrative leaders who sometimes feel they must compromise more than other leaders. Any that you could not answer yes to should become your goals as you study this book.

List your leadership goals below: For instance, "I will look for opportunities to be more decisive."

Goal 1: _____

_____

Goal 2: _____

_____

Goal 3: _____

_____

Goal 4: _____

_____

Goal 5: _____

_____

Adapted from Leadership Skills for Women, *by Marilyn Manning & Patricia Haddock, Crisp Publications, 1995.*

P A R T 2

Enhancing Your Professional Image

Assessing Your Image

"I am a very important part of my manager's administrative team who can be relied on in any emergency." (An administrator quoted in Working Woman *magazine*)

"My administrator is a sales representative, customer-service expert, quality-control inspector, data-processing coordinator, and too many additional things to list here." (A company vice president quoted in the same article)

Are you harvesting the highest personal growth potential from your job?

How do you see yourself in your job?

How do others see you?

Flexibility is a key quality in meeting your manager's and organization's ever-changing needs. Each day, pressures and adjustments will require your ability to reprioritize in order to complete the most important tasks. In time, within the framework of your particular job, you will develop your own areas of expertise. Chances are, you will find your job responsibilities growing at the same rate as your personal confidence level. You are a key player on the office team. You are often the one who really "makes things happen."

The following profiles are all true stories. Which is most like you?

BRAD, MELISSA, JUANITA

Brad's office skills are adequate, although his writing and spelling ability is poor. He hangs a comic "calendar" over his desk. It shows sleeping figures in the boxes for Monday through Thursday, and laughing, happy figures on Friday, Saturday, and Sunday. On his computer, he places a little statue holding a flag that says, "Think Friday." He's often 15 or 20 minutes late in the morning. He always seems to have an "excuse." When given added responsibilities, he doesn't finish on time or do a complete job, unless someone reminds and prods him. He avoids volunteering for additional duties. He complains that he would like a more interesting job and better pay.

What advice would you give to Brad?

Re evaluate the image you are projecting to your co-workers.
Learn to follow through on current responsibilities & finish what you start.
Work on being dependable and available to help others.

Melissa did not work outside of her home for 12 years while her children were young. Once she decided to return to the workplace she attended the local community college to update her office skills. Once she felt confident with her basic skills she began interviewing for a job and was soon hired by a local realty firm. She wants to eventually study for a real-estate license and has already begun to take courses.

How could Melissa manage her job to achieve her personal goals?

Learn on the job - helps to prepare for exam for license. Observe others - How they handle situations - gives experience.

Would these changes improve or detract from her professional image in her present job? Why?

Improve - Shows initative to learn

CONTINUED

Juanita decided to accept a job in a bank because she always enjoyed working with figures and was intrigued with investments. She started as a temp at the headquarters of an international bank and became a permanent employee after six months. In the past eight years, she has worked in virtually every department of the bank. She is currently the assistant to the president, supervising an elegant two-floor suite that was filmed in a James Bond movie. She composes and types most of the president's letters and memos. She has developed a sizable investment portfolio, based on opportunities discovered through her research for bank reports.

Was Juanita just lucky? List some of the traits that enabled her to rise to her current position in the organization.

No - Had interest in learning different areas of the bank which helped her move up into new positions at the bank as well as benefit her investment portfolio by what she learned.

Dedication, Hard work, Willingness to Learn

Taking Stock

Brad, Melissa, and Juanita all started with the same general job description, but each person chose individual goals and attitudes. How can you manage your job to best meet your personal goals?

First you have to assess what they are. Below are some questions to get you started. Remember: be honest with yourself. No one else will be affected by your answers but you.

Yes No

☑ ❑ Do you have a clear vision of where you are going with your professional and personal life during the next five years?

☑ ❑ Do others know about your plans?

☑ ❑ Have you set specific measurable goals for the next one to five years?

☑ ❑ Do those in your support system know about these targets?

☑ ❑ Are you totally satisfied with your progress in your professional life?

☑ ❑ Are you satisfied with your life progress?

❑ ❑ Do you track your professional and personal progress?

❑ ❑ Have you articulated your values?

❑ ❑ Have you written them down?

Because an administrative position is usually flexible, within certain limitations, you have the power to make your job work for you. You can test and challenge yourself and grow professionally and personally.

The Benefits of a Professional Image

Many good things can happen once you realize your potential. Of the nine statements listed below, three are false. Place a check (✔) in the square opposite the false statements and match your answers with those at the bottom of the page.

With greater professionalism I will:

❑ 1. Increase my promotion and earnings potential.

❑ 2. Have opportunities to learn more skills.

☑ 3. Develop too much stress.

☑ 4. Have less freedom.

❑ 5. Increase my self-confidence.

❑ 6. Try out my leadership wings.

☑ 7. Have fewer friends.

❑ 8. Learn and develop human relations skills.

❑ 9. Have better feelings of self-worth.

False Statements

3. There is no evidence that top-flight professionals have more stress than other employees.

4. Professional administrators generally have more freedom, because their managers trust them with far more authority.

7. Professionals develop new friends and keep the old ones.

Adapted from The New Supervisor, *by Elwood N. Chapman, Crisp Publications, 1992.*

Updating Your Office Skills

When you view yourself as an office professional, your fields of study can lead in exciting new directions. Your expertise should begin with a basic mastery of office skills, but can go far beyond. Whatever your background, chances are there are new procedures and skills that would help you do a better job.

Consider the following areas when you explore office or college course descriptions:

➤ Office Administration

➤ Office Technology and Applications Software

➤ Business Economics

➤ Financial Analysis and Management

➤ Marketing

➤ Management

➤ Accounting

➤ Business Law

➤ Communications (Speaking, Writing) *B , J*

Many companies have programs that pay tuition costs for employees who take courses and workshops. Large organizations often offer in-house training programs on a regular basis. Or you may find just the class you need on the Internet.

Do you know what educational opportunities your employer offers? Are you aware of classes that would help you professionally that are available at your local schools and colleges? Be a decision maker and problem solver. Look for classes to enhance your skills. Don't forget to give yourself credit for reading this book.

Becoming More Marketable

As your professional skills grow, it is normal for you to see yourself differently. Your outward appearance and personal habits may change. This section will provide some examples of "finishing touches" that make the difference in realizing your potential.

Personal Appearance

The first thing anyone notices about you is how you look. We all know, too, that how we look affects how we feel. Our self-image definitely influences our attitude. To become a professional success, look like a success every day. You never have a second chance to make a first impression.

The specifics of appropriate appearance vary from place to place, year by year. But you can always observe professionally dressed people in your own office or on the street, making note of which styles seem appropriate for you. (Also observe those details that label a person as unprofessional.) Consider how you can use the following elements to enhance the image you want to project:

➤ Simplicity

➤ Elegance

➤ Orderliness

These elements apply to your hairstyle as well as your clothing. Your clothes make a statement about you. Dress the part you would like to play in your professional world.

At this point, you may wonder if you have to throw out everything you now own. Certainly not. But don't wear inappropriate clothing to the office.

Looking Professional

How to Sabotage Your Image:

➤ Buy cheap clothing

➤ Wear worn-out or soiled clothing

➤ Look sloppy

➤ Dress immaturely

➤ Disregard your grooming

➤ Wear inappropriate accessories—things that stand out garishly

➤ Dress inappropriately for the occasion or your age

➤ Ignore your personal habits and hygiene (gum chewing, body odor, bad breath, etc.)

➤ Follow the latest fashion trends blindly

How Not to Sabotage Your Image:

➤ Wear clean, pressed clothing

➤ Go for a neat and tidy look—tuck in shirttails

➤ Buy clothing that fits properly, not too tight

➤ Accessorize modestly

➤ Stick to classics and avoid trends

Remember that simplicity and professionalism in your image enhances your marketability.

Non-Verbal Communication or Body Language

It has been proven that 65% of all communication is non-verbal. This is what others remember about you long after they have forgotten what you said.

Think about the following elements and observe the people in your own office. Then, pledge that for the rest of your working life, you will make your non-verbal communication say "professional."

➤ **Handshake**
Both men and women should have a firm, steady handshake. This shows self-confidence and a willingness to communicate.

➤ **Appropriate or Inappropriate Laughter**
Laughter is a very individual trait. In general, however, it is better to curtail loud horselaughs and foolish giggling in a business setting. Excessive laughter usually indicates nervousness.

➤ **Facial Expressions**
"Eye rolling" and "wide-eyed child" faces grow tiresome very quickly.

➤ **Rate of Speech**
Slower is better than faster, especially on the telephone.

➤ **Posture**
The professional person looks calm, relaxed, yet ready for work and challenge. This means standing, sitting, and moving with grace. Don't slouch, twist, or contort yourself.

➤ **Gestures**
These can emphasize your point when appropriate, but too many gestures can make other people uncomfortable.

➤ **Eye Contact**
Maintain eye contact with the person to whom you are speaking. If you are sitting, turn around and face the person fully.

Your image is a picture, a portrait. What you wear, say, and do forms an overall impression—make yours professional.

Remaining Politically Correct

It can be difficult for even the most skilled politician to act "correctly" in difficult situations. But as any politician can confirm, insensitive blunders are quite hard to recover from.

Situations that require careful consideration and tactful responses might include:

➤ Supporting your manager when you know he or she is wrong

➤ Being made the scapegoat for your manager's mistakes

➤ When someone shares negative gossip with you

➤ Having someone at the "top" ask you to do something you don't agree with

➤ Being asked to correct a co-worker's mistake

➤ When a friend and co-worker asks you to share confidential information

➤ Saying the wrong thing in an important meeting

➤ Having someone else take credit for your idea

➤ Knowing something that could harm a project or your company

➤ Being asked to support promotions for people when you know they cannot do the job

Which of the above have you faced? What have you learned from these situations? What decisions have you made to face these future challenges?

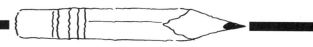

HOW MARKETABLE ARE YOU?

Check (✔) True or False for each statement.

True False

☑ ☐ The first thing anyone notices about you is how you look.

☐ ☑ It's okay to wear sports clothes on the days the boss won't be in the office.

☐ ☑ You should throw out any unprofessional clothes in your closet.

☐ ☑ It's always safe to follow the latest fashion trends.

☐ ☑ If you are discreet, it is okay to chew gum and/or eat "munchies" at your desk.

☐ ☑ You don't need a firm handshake.

☐ ☑ The faster your rate of speaking, the more businesslike you sound.

☐ ☑ When speaking to someone, look over the person's shoulder to avoid embarrassment.

☐ ☑ On your first day of work, bring a box of personal possessions to decorate your own space.

☑ ☐ Your professional image is a portrait of how you look, speak, and behave.

Answers: The first and last statements are true. The rest are false.

P A R T 3

Expanding
Your Skills

Enhancing Your Role

Whether your office consists of just you and your manager or a large number of people, your office-managing skills will set the climate for everyone. You can help others achieve better performance.

You are especially valuable to your organization because you juggle many tasks at once. Computers and office technology will never make your job obsolete. Single-task occupations can be phased out, but the diverse role of an administrative professional remains vital and dynamic.

Your administrative role requires you to establish priorities, coordinate projects, and organize resources. As an office coordinator, your professional attitude and behavior greatly influence each day's accomplishments.

Prioritizing Work Overload

Do you often feel overloaded with work? If so, a major reason may be that your manager does not understand how long certain tasks take, or may be unaware of other duties that must be performed at the same time.

When you view work overload as a challenge, rather than a problem, solutions will come more easily. If you do not communicate (and document) the problem, however, your overload will become the rule and not the exception. Make sure you discuss overload problems with your manager after you have done the following:

➤ Keep a written record of work requests, deadlines, time approximations vs. time actually spent

➤ If your supervisor interrupts you with new work requests, negotiate the deadlines

➤ Ask for outside help when you need it

➤ Do not hesitate to ask questions about deadlines or priorities

✳ One of your biggest frustrations may be the lack of time with your manager. It's essential to have quality time together.

Tips for Meeting with Your Manager

➤ Request and plan for regular meetings with your manager. Ad hoc meetings are useful but not a substitute.

➤ Keep it short. Thirty minutes every week might work.

➤ Make it "your" meeting with your agenda.

➤ Follow your prioritized agenda.

➤ Bring solutions and important questions.

➤ Speak concisely. Give details that are absolutely essential.

➤ Listen.

➤ Summarize. Reconfirm what decisions you have made together.

The first step toward control of your managerial duties is to list all of your office tasks and then rate them. Use the chart on the next page to determine your priorities.

Setting Priorities

Identify and then list your tasks and activities at work. If you have difficulty remembering them, just close your eyes and envision yourself in your work space doing your job. Notice the various tasks and activities. Do you answer the phone? Complete forms? Answer letters? List them below.

Task	Impact	Priority

Rate Impact: Using a scale from 1 to 10, with 1 being "no impact" and 10 being "great impact," rate the impact that each activity has upon performance of your job.

Assign Priorities: Use the impact ratings to assign priorities to each task or activity. Assign an "A" priority for tasks with ratings over 7; "B" priority for ratings from 4 to 6; and "C" priority for ratings below 3.

Schedule: Use your priority-rating system to schedule your day. Start with "A" tasks and activities. Try scheduling them directly on your calendar. Leave "C" priorities until last and, whenever possible, delegate them. What would happen if you didn't do the "C" activity at all?

Task	Impact	Priority
Keeping correspondence filed in chronological order.	7	A

Discuss your opinions with your manager and ask for ideas about the best use of your time.

Rating sheet adapted from Preventing Job Burnout, *Revised Edition, by Beverly A. Potter, Ph.D., Crisp Publications, 1996.*

Time-Management Tips

Successful professionals are expert time managers. To reach your goals, you must prioritize responsibilities, finish tasks completely, and create schedules—and stick to them.

Secrets of Time Management

➤ Do top-priority tasks first, when you have high energy.

➤ Save routine tasks for your low-energy time of day.

➤ Divide big jobs into manageable steps.

➤ Use a timetable: daily, weekly, and monthly.

➤ Finish tasks completely (or use very good notes to yourself so that you don't waste time when you return).

➤ Use telephone time wisely. Have and take notes. Assert to end conversations. Schedule call-backs.

MARK AND THE PROMOTION REPORT

Mark, as assistant to the vice president in charge of marketing, was asked to prepare a report summarizing the results of the last three years from a promotion letter sent each spring and recommending changes to this year's letter. Mark has the necessary research materials filed in the office, but somehow has not found the right moment to start the report. Now there are only three weeks before the promotion letter should be sent out.

What should Mark do?

Block time and start on Report

GROUPING ACTIVITIES

When you consider your daily schedule, you may find that it reflects your past experience at another job. Or perhaps it developed by chance as you learned your present job. One exercise that will help you reevaluate your schedule is to imagine explaining your routine to an inexperienced visitor. Does it make sense? Have you ever really considered why you do certain things at certain times of the day? Following are some ideas that may make you more efficient.

Group Tasks for Greater Efficiency:

1. Schedule outgoing messages (phone, fax, email) in groups. Make notes about responses and/or any follow-up action that is required.

2. Sort and prioritize messages and correspondence into specific groups (e.g. immediate action by boss, "I can handle," information, junk, etc.).

3. Draft replies immediately.

4. Stock supplies once a week, rather than running to the supply closet or requisitioning items every day.

5. If you have assistants, give them all their work and instructions at one time, rather than for each separate job. Set a regular time to meet with them.

6. Prepare the outgoing mail throughout the day rather than leaving it all until the last minute and perhaps missing the last pickup.

7. Make a checklist and organize every step of a major mailing at one time, so that all necessary letterhead, forms, envelopes, enclosures, etc., can be ordered simultaneously.

8. At the end of each day, take a few minutes to organize a To-Do list for the following day, with subjects such as: Mail (email and "snail mail"), Report, Telephone Calls, Appointments, Internal Follow-ups.

Identify Your Stressors

As hard as you try to organize your schedule and time, the demands to do more with less keep increasing. It helps to take stock of what adds to your stress so that you can plan ways to minimize negative impacts. Identify your stressors so you better manage your time.

Which of these cause you stress?

➤ Constant interruptions

➤ Having to come in early, work late, or work on weekends

➤ People asking for things at the last minute

➤ The lack of predictable blocks of uninterrupted time each day

➤ People asking redundant questions

➤ Someone who seldom returns phone calls or emails *Set Deadline for Answer for*

➤ The lack of meeting time with your manager *give reason for needing answer*

➤ Irrelevant emails and messages *Delete*

➤ The messy condition of your work area

Set three goals that address your stressors:

For example: I will schedule a short weekly meeting with my manager.

Goal 1: *Schedule wkly meeting with Jay*

Goal 2: _____

Goal 3: _____

Turn Your Telephone into a Time-Management Tool

Interruptions are hard to control, and the phone is the biggest offender. Let your telephone work for you, rather than control you:

➤ Assert yourself to end calls tactfully. Don't let the other person control your time.

➤ Tell the caller before you transfer a call: "Here's the number in case you get cut off."

➤ Before you make a call, make notes about the key points.

➤ Make your follow-up notes during the phone call.

➤ Control "small talk" and get to the purpose of the call quickly.

➤ If someone wanders from the point, mention a word from their comments to bridge back to the point.

Your Ideas for a Different Work Schedule

Consider your stressors when you think creatively about your schedule. See if you can redesign how you use your day. This may not always be possible, but give it a try to see if it helps you control your time better.

1. Tasks that should be done in the first hour:

   Emails, phone calls / Voice Mail / Calendars

2. Tasks for the half-hour before lunch:

3. Tasks for immediately after lunch:

4. End-of-the-day tasks:

Long-Range Planning

Think like a manager. Office activities should be anticipated, planned, and coordinated on a long-range basis. The overall pattern of your job should be structured to be congruent with your manager's long-term goals.

You and your manager must work together on this. Only by becoming active partners and communicating objectives and needs will you be in a position to actualize your goals.

Set the Scene for Long-Range Planning

1. Make a list of reports or projects that occur annually, semi-annually, quarterly, monthly, and weekly. Put this information on a calendar or timeline chart.

2. Indicate time periods on the chart that are normally hectic.

3. Note any scheduled trips, vacation periods, holidays, etc.

4. Fill in regular meetings and appointments that can be predicted.

5. Once you have completed 1-4, you should have a "year-at-a-glance" planning document.

6. Insist on periodic long-range planning sessions with your manager. A meeting, or series of meetings, between the two of you can assign priorities and establish schedules and deadlines.

7. Monthly and weekly planning will provide a realistic look at major activities and minimize the last-minute "frantics."

   What are the best times for you and your manager to plan or review long-range goals? _____

   Have you scheduled a meeting to discuss them? _____

   List all major long-range goals the office needs to consider and accomplish:

   _____

   _____

   What steps must you take to transform three of the major long-range goals into reality?

   _____

   _____

Using Project-Management Techniques

Increasing your project-management skills will make you more marketable. Project management is having a plan that meets goals within cost, schedule, and quality objectives. It optimizes resources and takes the skills, talents, and cooperative effort of a team to complete. Find opportunities to take leadership roles in projects.

How Do You Rate as a Project Manager?

Are you developed in the following skill areas?

1. Organizing a project from beginning to end

2. Enrolling and motivating

3. Setting measurable objectives and goals

4. Problem solving

5. Maximizing resources and minimizing waste

6. Measuring performance, creating benchmarking

If you have skills in five of these six areas, you should be volunteering to coordinate more projects. You may want to enroll in a project-management workshop to sharpen your skills.

Planning Steps

Key steps to consider in planning any major project are:

1. Establish the objective

2. Choose a basic strategy

3. Break the project down into steps and timelines

4. Outline the performance standards for each step

5. Set the correct sequence for the steps

6. Estimate the cost of the total project and each phase

7. Determine the staffing and resource needs

8. Identify what training is needed

9. Develop policies and procedures for the team members

Here's a Project Checklist to help keep you organized:

❑ Define the project scope and key strategies

❑ Develop a schedule and budget

❑ Assign decision-making authority and roles

❑ Provide training

❑ Monitor progress and make corrections

❑ Conduct team reviews

❑ Draft project report

❑ Finalize report

Develop your own templates and checklists to help you and your manager complete projects even more efficiently.

Decision Making in Six Easy Steps

Don't be afraid to make decisions. The types of decisions you make may be different from those a manager or a company president makes, but the process is identical. If a person understands the process, she or he can make quality decisions. If you are decisive, you are much more valuable to your organization.

Following are six steps to better decision making, along with examples illustrating each step:

1. Gather Information.

Be well-informed. Learn the facts. Talk to other people.

Example: Jennie needed to decide which of two software programs would handle the travel records. She asked other departments and other contacts for their recommendations. She read reviews of each program and kept notes of her findings.

2. Identify Options.

Which facts are relevant to the situation? What are this organization's values?

For instance, is saving money on equipment more important than getting the latest refinements? How many people will use this particular program and how skilled are they?

3. Test Each Option against the Situation.

Example: If Jennie bought one program, it would not run on all the computers in her office. If she bought the other program, it could not accommodate all of the categories she needed to record. Neither program fulfilled all of her office needs.

4. Make a Decision, Inform Others, and Note Who Is Responsible.
Inform those directly involved about the decision, summarizing the pros and cons.

Example: Jennie elected to select the program that could accommodate all of the needed travel categories.

5. Take Action on Your Decision.

Example: Jennie's purchase illustrates taking action on the decision.

6. Build in Feedback Vehicles to Assess the Effectiveness.

Example: Jennie can survey staff before and after the change.

Rate Your Decision-Making Skills

Describe a decision you made recently.

Asking to attend an administrative leadership training for Personal development as well as gathering information to bring training to the other admins here at our company site

Did you gather information?

Gathered information from the Catalog of training being offered by our Company as well as information brochure handed out at the training By the Company who Conducted the training

Did you evaluate the information?

I evaluated the information from the descriptions given for each level of training against other training Being offered by other Companies

What options did you consider?

Considered the option of going to the 5 series against a one time training - Evaluated Cost and content as well as the feasibility of bringing the training to our site

How did you recognize the consequences of each option? Explain.

By BRINGING training here - More admins would have the opportunity to attend as opposed to attending off-site training where only a few admins Could attend.

Did you inform others of your decision?

I met with our admin career development Committee and a representative from HR to discuss my experience in ATTENDING the training

What (if anything) do you plan to do differently with your next decision?

Go Directly to the person who Can make a decision

_____

Do you feel you are making more important decisions now than you were last year? Why?

YES - I WAS NOT in a position to attend or recommend this training even though I had given the information to a Committee to LOOK AT.

The more decisions you make, the greater your skill and self-confidence. Learn to tolerate more risks by being decisive and asserting your opinions.

This year I was able to Not only attend but to bring back information and personal experiences to share which Lends more Credibility

DECISION-MAKING CHECKLIST

Use the format below to help you make your next decision.

Decision to be made:_____

❑ I will gather information from:

People

Other sources

Others: _____

❑ I will evaluate the information by:

Checking its relevancy and my values and considering timing needs

Others: _____

❑ The consequences of each of my options are:

Option 1 _____

Option 2 _____

Option 3 _____

❑ I will communicate my decision to:

_____

_____

❑ I will follow up by:

_____

_____

When you have difficulty making a decision at the office, refer to this page and follow these steps. Remember: Every decision you make doesn't have to be perfect.

Communicating

for Results

Communication Skills

The first three topics in this section are of special importance because they reflect the times you are the voice of your organization. When you send messages, speak on the telephone, or make presentations, you represent your organization. By assessing your present level of confidence in these areas, you can identify where additional study and practice would be helpful. Good communication skills make every other part of your job easier.

Keep these general principles in mind whenever you are writing or speaking:

➤ There is no substitute for knowing the facts about your subject. Learn everything you can about your organization, how it works, who does what job, normal schedules and procedures, general policies, and which customers or clients warrant special consideration.

➤ Never be afraid to say or write that you do not know something. Do say, however, that you will find out and let the other person know as soon as possible. Then be sure to follow through on your promise.

➤ Always try to understand the other person's point of view: what is he or she really asking? Listen to the other person or read his or her message carefully, and consider the context from which it was written.

➤ When unpleasant information must be communicated, soften it with something positive.

➤ Observe how effective people around you use the telephone. Ask to read samples of their memos (including letters and emails). What works well for them? How could you adapt their methods to work for you?

Writing with Confidence

Many managers and executives understand that the highest-paid administrators are among the world's best ghostwriters. The better your communication skills (especially writing), the more time you save your manager and the more valuable you become. Rate yourself as a writer by answering the following questions:

Yes **No**

☑ ❏ I always keep my audience in mind when I write. Do they want to know every fact or just the "bottom line"? Are there cultural issues?

☑ ❏ I have no problem with the basics: grammar, spelling, and punctuation. (If your answer is "no," buy a handbook and dictionary and take a brush-up class.)

☑ ❏ I know the difference between active and passive construction, and try to use the active wherever possible. (Examples: Passive—The temp was hired by Mary. Active—Mary hired the temp.)

☑ ❏ I choose simple words to communicate clearly. (Examples: Complex—Subsequently, we'll require your endorsement. Simple—Later, we'll need your signature.)

☑ ❏ I make it a point to state clearly the specific purpose of my letters or memos. Preferably, in simple words in the first paragraph.

☑ ❏ I keep a file of sample letters and memos so I can quickly put together an appropriate response to the routine requests we receive.

❏ ❏ I personalize letters and memos so the recipient will feel recognized.

☑ ❏ If there is any doubt about how a name is spelled, I double-check it. I understand how important a person's name and title is.

☑ ❏ I know that it is hard to proofread my own work, so I have a "buddy" in the office with whom I exchange important letters, reports, etc.

Every "yes" makes you a better business writer.

A PLAN FOR WRITING

Planning before you write will keep you focused. Following is a checklist of questions to ask before you write any document, memo, or presentation.

Planning Checklist

1. Title or topic:_____

2. Specific outcome(s) desired:_____

3. Who are the readers?_____

4. The readers' knowledge of the topic and technical terminology is:

   ❑ high   ❑ low   ❑ mixed   ❑ unknown

5. After reading the document, the action(s) I want the readers to take is/are:

   _____

   _____

6. The readers probably have the following needs or concerns:_____

   _____

   _____

Writing Emails

Emails can be efficient ways to communicate, but if misused can be big time wasters. Are you becoming a "slave" to emails or taking control?

To make the most of email technology, consider the following:

➤ Beware of confidential subjects. Your messages may be forwarded, even if marked confidential.

➤ Know how you think. Maybe you're most efficient when you brainstorm and organize on paper first, then write the email. Paper is still okay and can save you from sending a hastily prepared email.

➤ Set high standards. Many readers are put off by bad writing in any form, email as well as hard copy.

➤ Select your readers carefully. Send copies only to those who need to see the message.

➤ Don't assume what you see on your screen is what your reader sees. If your readers' computer systems are different from yours, your line lengths cause an annoying text-wrap effect on their screens. To be safe, keep your lines to 55 or 60 characters, including spaces. Exaggerate any indentation you use to make sure it "catches" on your readers' screens.

➤ Avoid typing in all capitals. It's easier to type but IT SOUNDS LIKE SHOUTING. "All cap" writing slows reading by inhibiting recognition of acronyms, proper names, and sentence starts, which all depend on the contrasts between upper and lower case.

➤ Use informative subject lines. We often screen our emails by scanning subject lines. Readers may discard (without reading) messages that don't seem relevant or clear. To get your emails read, use "Request to reschedule meeting" or "How Project XYZ will save $500K per year." These specific subject lines communicate, even if the recipient doesn't read your whole email.

➤ Keep your email messages short.

➤ If you can't keep it short, forecast the structure. On your readers' first screen, summarize your message and then forecast its structure by listing all your section headings.

➤ Use emphasis devices. You can facilitate reading by using headings, white space, occasional all caps, indents, lists, simulated underlines, and other devices.

➤ <u>Beware of acronyms</u>.

➤ Don't overuse email jargon or those cute little "emotions" like :-(. Even though they can communicate quickly, make sure your readers accept them before you use them.

➤ Print out long emails. This will make it easier to scan for important sections than if you scroll on the screen.

➤ Reply quickly to your messages.

➤ Don't negate one of the main advantages of email—speed. Check your email frequently and reply promptly.

➤ Change the subject line of your reply, if you can. Reply to "Request to reschedule meeting" with "Meeting rescheduled to May 31," or respond to "How Project XYZ will save $500K per year" with "Okay, I'm sold: Let's do Project XYZ."

Adapted from 50 One-Minute Tips to Better Communication, *by Philip Bozek, Crisp Publications, 1998.*

Make Every Letter a Sales Letter

The cost to an organization of an original one-page letter is estimated at more than $20 when all office expenses are considered. It is therefore very important to make sure that your letters are professional in content and appearance and support your organization.

Every letter that leaves your office is a "Sales Letter." This is because it represents your manager or your company. You can make or break important future business by the way you handle written correspondence.

What Makes a Bad Letter?

Here are 10 easy ways to make a letter reader really mad:

1. Ramble around the subject so it's difficult to tell what the letter is trying to say

2. Fail to answer any questions asked in a previous letter

3. Spell the recipient's name wrong; get the address scrambled; assume an incorrect title or gender; or be too "familiar"

4. Sound demanding, selfish, or superior, or talk down to your reader

5. Use cliché after cliché, with nothing original or personal

6. Forget to send a reply card or return envelope when you request a quick answer

7. Don't provide a telephone number when you ask for a return call

8. Use small-sized or faintly printed type, so your letter is a real strain to read

9. Make your letter too long, with key points buried

10. Neglect to have someone proofread your letter

Take your letter-writing very seriously. To the reader, you are your organization.

Conveying Bad News Tactfully

Often in business we must break bad news to good people. This is one time where brevity takes a back seat to tact. Tone is important. Choose your words carefully; select words that are courteous and positive. Don't use qualifiers, passive construction, or euphemisms to avoid accepting responsibility.

For example, a company president wrote the following to her employees:

It is necessary to resize our operation to the level of profitable market opportunities.

What she meant was this:

We must lay off staff.

Note the difference between the following positive and negative phrases:

Negative:	**Positive:**
You failed to notice…	May I point out that…
You neglected to mention…	We also can consider…
You overlooked the fact…	One additional fact is…
You missed the point…	From another perspective…
If you persist in…	If you choose to…
I see no alternative but…	Our clear plan of action…

How to Say No

At times we must deny an employee's request. Be direct and considerate, but don't be too subtle; otherwise, you may mislead by offering false hope instead of communicating clearly. Remember: even criticism can be delivered positively.

Two excellent self-study books on business writing are Better Business Writing, *by Susan L. Brock, Crisp Publications, 1996, and* Writing Fitness, *by Jack Swenson, Crisp Publications, 1988.*

How Well Do You Listen?

Listening is probably the most important communication skill you can improve. Try these practical tips:

Tips for Better Listening

➤ Take notes.

➤ Listen and repeat. When you repeat what you heard you tend to remember.

➤ Demonstrate that you want to listen. Show desire, interest, and focus.

➤ Be present. Stop your mind from wandering.

➤ Keep a positive outlook.

➤ Become a "total" listener. Use your ears, eyes, and mind.

➤ Build rapport by matching the speakers gestures, expressions, and voice patterns, if appropriate.

➤ Monitor your "hot buttons" —know what makes you angry.

➤ Control distractions (e.g., turn off cell phone, pager)

When you are listening and responding, choosing the correct words can make a real difference. Show the speaker that you are open-minded and receptive.

Avoid:	Use instead:
"You should have . . . "	*"Will you please . . ."*
"I'll try . . . "	*"I will . . ."*
"You made a mistake"	*"Will you please . . . "*
"Your complaint"	*"Your question"*
"Your problem"	*"This situation"*
"You can't . . ."	*"You can . . ."*
"We can't . . ."	*"You can . . ."*
"As soon as possible"	*"Before _____ o'clock"*
"I'm just . . ."	*"I am . . ."*
"There's nothing I can do"	*"I will _____ (list actions)"*
"Why didn't you . . . "	*"Will you please . . ."*

Adapted from Telephone and Time Management, *by Dru Scott, Crisp Publications, 1988.*

Effective Presentation Skills

Administrators have many opportunities for oral communication. For example, attending a meeting, hosting visiting salespeople, or explaining your duties to trainees can lead to public speaking in many different settings. Following is a typical example of presenting information to a group of colleagues.

JILL AND THE IMPROMPTU SPEECH

Jill is invited, along with her manager, to attend a meeting of all department heads in the company. She is not expecting to say anything, only to sit and listen. During her manager's presentation, he is asked a question about the department's plans for the coming year. He turns to Jill and says, "Jill, you've been working on this project while I've been away. Maybe you could say a few words about how this project got started, where it stands, and where it is going."

If something like this happens to you, don't panic. You know how to organize your thoughts and you know your job. With these two resources you can effectively respond by taking the following steps:

➤ First, think.

Use your organizational skills. Any topic can be split into components. Before you speak, break your topic into a pattern such as:

➤ Past, present, and future (or any time-oriented combination)

➤ Topic 1, 2, and 3 (e.g., production, advertising, and marketing)

➤ The pros and cons of an issue (useful in persuasive situations)

In Jill's case above, the time-ordered sequence fits right in.

➤ Then, speak.

When asked to speak unexpectedly

1. Give a few introductory remarks.

Give yourself time to get organized. Make some general introductory comments, such as, "Thanks, I'm pleased to be here today to help provide some information. I didn't plan a formal presentation but would be happy to describe the project we've been working on." Do not apologize for not having a prepared speech.

2. Develop a clear preview sentence of your main points.

Verbalize to yourself and your audience what your key points are. From the example above Jill could simply state, "I would like to tell you about how we started this project, where it stands, and where we plan to take it." This is a time-ordered sequence.

3. Deliver the body of the presentation.

Talk through each point from your preview sentence. (In Jill's example; past, present, and future). Establishing an organizational pattern and knowing where you are going will take some of the stress out of the situation. If what you are speaking about is controversial, first acknowledge the opposition's case and follow with your viewpoint so you end by summarizing your position.

4. Review the main points.

Reinforce the main ideas by briefly restating them. Something like, "I've tried in these past few minutes to give you an overview of how this project started, where it is now, and where we think it will go."

5. Conclude the presentation.

Conclude with a strong, positive statement. Following our example, "I hope to attend next month's meeting to report a satisfactory conclusion to our project. I would be happy to take any questions at this time."

If you find yourself regularly being called upon to contribute at meetings, you will find many helpful ideas in *Effective Presentation Skills; A Practical Guide for Better Speaking, Revised Edition,* by Steve Mandel (Crisp Publications, 1993). The above impromptu speaking guide was adapted from this book.

Using Laptops and LCD Panels Effectively

If you give presentations with the help of laptop computers and/or liquid crystal display (LCD) panels, consider the following about this technology:

The Pros:

➤ Excellent graphics programs are available

➤ Striking visual effects are possible

➤ Electronic slides can be created quickly

➤ Programs can make slides, hard-copy overheads, outlines, and speaker's notes

➤ Using the technology lends high-tech credibility to the presenter

The Cons:

➤ Encourages a visual for every thought

➤ Requires special equipment

➤ May take a long time to set up or boot up

➤ Can detract attention from presenter

➤ May require dim room lighting

➤ Makes it easy to overdo visual effects

➤ May be hard to tailor on the fly

Tips for Using Laptops or LCDs:

➤ Don't overdo visual effects

➤ If possible, index slides for quick reference

➤ Have a back-up plan—a hard copy version of your slides

➤ Get there early; check everything twice

➤ If you are using a TV monitor, use at least a 27-inch screen

➤ Ensure that the image is large enough to be seen from the back of the room

➤ For long discussions on any slide, turn off the screen saver feature

➤ Use cascading bullets or progressive highlighting

➤ For commands, use a remote portable mouse

➤ Create a "dark slide" effect so you can occasionally speak without visual aids

Techniques for Videoconferencing

Videoconference presentations take special consideration. Learning to master these techniques can help you create more value to the team.

Before the presentation:

➤ Analyze your listeners. Plan for a strong presentation—brief, clear, and dynamic.

➤ Make your graphics large, bold, and simple, especially if your equipment shows graphics as a small "screen-in-screen" display. Consider using large table-top flipchart easels.

➤ Wear a light blue or pastel shirt or blouse—not a white one, which may cause camera flare and a medium dark or dark coat. Avoid patterned fabrics and flashy or noisy jewelry.

➤ Distribute and space the conference microphones properly. Preset the video shots and quick-zooms you plan to use.

➤ Obtain someone who can devote full attention to operating the video equipment. The presenter should not do it.

Kickoff:

➤ Set ground rules. Be specific about when you will accept questions.

➤ Make sure all participants are in the camera's view. People not on camera should not be allowed to talk.

During the presentation:

➤ Be expressive. Use your animated voice and face to make up for the faintness of body-language cues.

➤ Ensure comprehension by asking: "Am I being clear?" "Does that make sense so far?" or "Any questions?"

➤ Speak loudly, even if you are speaking to someone right next to you. Avoid side conversations, shuffling papers, tapping pencils, and other distractions.

➤ Monitor sound levels to avoid feedback and echoes.

➤ If possible, use the zoom lens to focus on whoever is speaking.

As with telephone conferences, you shouldn't expect results as good as those from live, face-to-face talks. In video conferences, both presenters and listeners usually are inhibited by video technology, and people inevitably feel somewhat disconnected.

Videoconferences work better when those involved know each other from previous live meetings. If you assemble a team to work together through frequent videoconferencing, try to get them together live now and then. No technology can compare to the power of real people, living in each other's presence, speaking, and using eye contact.

Adapted from 50 One-Minute Tips to Better Communication, *by Phillip E. Bozek, Crisp Publications, 1998.*

Planning for Meetings

Most leaders complain that meetings consume too much of their time. You can help your manager minimize time loss by good preplanning.

The next time you are planning a meeting consider the following:

➤ Set up a checklist of premeeting arrangements, such as room reservations, audio-visual rental, food requirements, and budget considerations.

➤ Send written announcements to all participants (with an enclosed agenda when possible).

➤ Enclose RSVP directions or a phone number.

➤ Be sure to follow up with phone calls if people have not replied by a certain date.

➤ Start collecting materials for the meeting. Sometimes it is helpful to have a large box, basket, or cart. Make a checklist of any necessary charts, reports, extra agendas, name tags and pens, blank notepads, your own note-taking necessities.

➤ Keep an up-to-date list of RSVPs and advise your manager of any feedback from others. These might include issues, "secret" agendas, desires for time or date change, and so on. The more your manager can anticipate in advance, the better.

➤ Plan to arrive early at the meeting site. Make sure that the room is clean, the temperature is comfortable, there are enough chairs, and all needed supplies are on hand. If your preplanning has been thorough, there should not be any surprises. However, something usually needs adjustment.

➤ Be sure to provide the number of your cell phone to someone in your office. (They may need to relay telephone calls to meeting participants.)

➤ As participants arrive, give them name tags and other appropriate materials.

➤ Be ready to supply anything further that your manager may need as the meeting progresses.

➤ Take notes, or have someone else do so.

➤ At an appropriate time following the meeting (e.g., the next day), sit down with your manager and discuss how a similar meeting could be even better next time.

➤ Keep a complete file on the meeting, including agenda, notes, lists of supplies, participants, and suggestions for improvement next time.

Planning and creating a successful meeting takes managerial talent, tact, and humor. This part of your job can be exhausting–but also the most fun.

For an excellent book on meetings, read Effective Meeting Skills, *by Elvin Haynes, Crisp Publications, 1997.*

Becoming an Effective Facilitator

As your role of administrator and coordinator expands, you will need excellent facilitation skills. You may be facilitating meetings for your manager and for projects you are involved with. Here are some tips to help you and your manager facilitate better.

Facilitation Tips

➤ Don't monopolize the discussion.

➤ Don't show verbal or non-verbal disapproval of ideas, even if you disagree with them.

➤ Frame problems as opportunities. Don't ask if it's possible to achieve a goal; ask "How can we achieve our goal?"

➤ Identify (to yourself) the introverts in the group and find ways to include them without putting them on the spot.

➤ Don't let extroverts monopolize.

➤ Don't let senior members of the group dominate.

➤ Use meeting procedures that require the participation of all.

➤ Probe to find out what's bothering those who exhibit "hostile silence."

➤ Change the initial seating arrangement, if necessary.

➤ Rotate leadership in standing meetings.

TEN KEY STATEMENTS FOR EFFECTIVE FACILITATION

Good facilitators contribute frequent short comments to direct the flow of meeting discussions. Here's a list of specific phrases you might use:

1. *"What about this . . . "*

   This could be a suggestion that the group try a new approach.

2. *"What are your thoughts?"*

   A request for input to one or more participants.

3. *"Let me restate that . . . "*

   An attempt to clarify what has just been said.

4. *"That builds on what Juan said."*

   Be complimentary of group members and link ideas.

5. *"Is that related?"*

   Always control wasteful digressions.

6. *"Be fair."*

   An attempt to encourage diplomacy.

7. *"Can we all live with that?"*

   An important consensus question.

8. *"Let's give everyone a chance to respond."*

   Help maintain order.

9. *"What are our key decisions?"*

   Summarizing periodically during the meeting is critical.

10. *"Let's review our goals and deadlines?"*

    Assign ownership and follow through of goals.

Silence is an important responsibility of a good facilitator. Monitor your own talking and make time available fairly to all participants.

When Your Manager Travels to a Meeting

Helping your manager prepare for a meeting away from the office is a breeze compared to the responsibility of hosting one. Use the following checklist both before and after a meeting, conference, or convention. With a definite system, you will avoid last-minute panic.

Before the trip or meeting:

❏ Start a folder for the trip as soon as you know one is scheduled.

❏ Collect information about meeting dates, transportation and/or lodging requirements, RSVP procedures, etc.

❏ Put in reminder slips of things your boss may wish to take along.

❏ Review contents of previous folders; check whether the same material is needed on this occasion.

❏ Make any necessary reservations for travel, meals, or lodging.

❏ Pretend you are "in your manager's shoes" and visualize what else might be needed.

❏ Make a list of everything taken to the meeting.

After the trip or meeting:

❏ Review how the meeting arrangements went with your boss.

❏ Ask if additional data was needed for the meeting. Was it something you could have anticipated?

❏ Keep a folder of handouts, the agenda of the meeting, etc. Take action on any items requiring follow-up or a response.

❏ Check returned items off the list you made of things taken to the meeting.

❏ File the meeting folder and the "things needed" lists.

Your manager will thank you for helping him or her organize conference papers. You both may need them later when planning long-term goals or writing reports and memos.

Building Relationships and Networks

Interpersonal Skills

In a recent study, The Research Institute of America reported that major career advancement for administrative professionals is based on interpersonal skills. Technical skills and effort, although essential, were considered less important than good interpersonal skills.

Your ability to work with other people is your most valuable asset. Surveys show that top administrators and coordinators have more contacts with people than any other individuals on the organization chart. This section presents a number of ways to improve your people-handling skills.

The basis for every skill in this section is your *attitude*.

To work well with others, you must feel good about yourself—and that feeling spreads outward, affecting everyone around you.

Of course, everyone has times when his or her attitude needs renewal, so a good place to start is with your attitude today.

Take out your pencil and take the attitude assessment on the next page.

ATTITUDE ASSESSMENT SCALE

Rate your current attitude. Read the statement and circle the number where you feel you belong. If you circle a 10, you are saying your attitude could not be better in this area; if you circle a 1, you are saying it could not be worse. Be honest.

10=High (Positive) 1=Low (Negative)

1. My feeling is that my manager would rate my attitude as:

   10   9   **(8)**   7   6   5   4   3   2   1

2. Given the same choice, my co-workers and family would rate my attitude as:

   10   **(9)**   8   7   6   5   4   3   2   1

3. Realistically, I would rate my attitude as:

   10   9   8   **(7)**   6   5   4   3   2   1

4. In dealing with others, I believe my effectiveness would rate:

   10   **(9)**   8   7   6   5   4   3   2   1

5. My current rating as a communicator is:

   10   **(9)**   8   7   6   5   4   3   2   1

6. If there were a meter that could gauge my sense of humor, I believe it would read:

   10   9   8   **(7)**   6   5   4   3   2   1

7. My recent disposition—the patience and sensitivity I show to others—deserves a rating of:

   10   **(9)**   8   7   6   5   4   3   2   1

CONTINUED

CONTINUED

8. When it comes to not allowing little things to bother me, I deserve a:

10   9   8   7   (6)   5   4   3   2   1

9. Based upon the number of compliments I have received lately, I deserve a:

10   9   8   (7)   6   5   4   3   2   1

10. I would rate my enthusiasm toward my job and life during the last few weeks as:

10   9   8   (7)   6   5   4   3   2   1

Total _____78_____

A score of 90 or over is a signal that your attitude is "in tune" and no adjustments seem necessary; a score between 70 and 90 indicates that minor adjustments may help; a rating between 50 and 70 suggests a major adjustment; if you rated yourself below 50, a complete overhaul may be required.

If the attitude assessment scale shows you areas that could be improved, read Attitude: Your Most Priceless Possession, *by Elwood N. Chapman and Wil McKnight, Crisp Publications, 2001.*

Understanding Your Personality

Dealing positively with other people depends on two aspects of personality:

➤ Assertiveness

➤ Receptiveness

When you understand yourself in these areas, you become more skillful in handling your many responsibilities at work. Ideally, the professional employee will keep a healthy balance between assertiveness and receptiveness.

Your assertiveness enables you to set priorities, organize your time and energies, and let others know that you are a serious professional. When you are active, direct, and honest, you communicate self-respect and respect for others. People know where you stand, and trust you to listen to their points of view.

Your receptiveness helps you listen and really hear what you need to know about other people's needs and priorities. Even when people say things that are critical or unpleasant, you maintain your poise and use the information to help you do a better job.

Assertiveness

Let's first look at assertiveness, which can be defined as being pleasantly direct.

Do not confuse assertiveness with aggressiveness. When you are assertive you are being honest. Your attitude is "this is important to me and I am entitled to my opinion. At the same time, I respect that you are also entitled to your opinion."

The very nature of your work involves juggling a variety of duties. By your honest and direct communication with everyone, you gain energy and do a better job.

HOW ASSERTIVE ARE YOU?

By honestly answering the following questions, you will better understand your attitude toward assertiveness. An attitude, of course, does not always show up in behavior. You may feel more assertive than you are in real-life situations.

True False

1. ❏ ☑ **1.** I often feel like telling people what I really think of them.

2. ☑ ❏ **2.** When I find myself in a new situation, I watch what other people do and then try to act in a similar fashion.

3. ❏ ☑ **3.** I enjoy doing things that others may regard as controversial.

4. ☑ ❏ **4.** I think it is important to learn and practice correct social behavior.

5. ☑ ❏ **5.** In general, I find that I dislike nonconformists.

6. ☑ ❏ **6.** I prefer to listen to the opinions of others before I take a stand.

7. ☑ ❏ **7.** I feel comfortable following instructions and doing what is expected of me.

8. ❏ ☑ **8.** It often makes more sense to go along with "the group" rather than try to persuade them to my point of view.

9. ☑ ❏ **9.** Confronting other people is extremely uncomfortable for me.

10. ❏ ☑ **10.** I enjoy being seen as a person with strong opinions.

If you answered True to items 2, 4, 5, 6, 7, 8, or 9, give yourself one point for each. Also give one point for False answers to items 1, 3, or 10, and total your points. If you scored 6 or more points, low assertiveness may be a problem for you. You may find yourself being far more reactive to the demands of others than you are to your own aspirations.

A good book on assertiveness is Developing Positive Assertiveness, *by Sam Lloyd, Crisp Publications, 2001.*

Receptiveness

Receptiveness means being open to feedback. Obtaining feedback, even from your most severe critic, may be the most important way for you to gain direction and control. This feedback can lead to greater self-understanding and personal growth. Read the following case study and respond to the questions.

KERI AND BRITNEY

Keri, while eating lunch with her good friend Britney, got on the subject of constructive criticism. Keri confided to Britney that she was having difficulty understanding why her relationship with her boyfriend didn't seem to be going anywhere.

"If only he'd say what it is about me that doesn't appeal to him. I'd work on changing," Keri said, "but he just won't say. You're an old friend, Britney. What do you think I'm doing wrong?"

Britney had been waiting for this. Keri is a great person but has some irritating behaviors. For example, she spends too much time complaining about things but doesn't seem to make any changes to make things better. So, what the heck, Britney thought, I'll tell her now while she seems to be looking for feedback.

"Keri," Britney began, "You do have one trait that I find irritating, and maybe it bugs your boyfriend, too. You do an awful lot of complaining."

There was no response and Britney thought Keri didn't seem too upset by what she'd said, so she continued: "In fact, it can be very depressing to be around you, because you always seem to complain about the same things—your boyfriend, your mother, your car—and yet you never seem to do anything to make things better. What I'd like to hear are some good things or some positive plans."

Keri still wasn't responding and didn't even seem mad. After a pause, she started laughing out loud.

Then she said, "Britney, do you realize that you just described perfectly your own habit of complaining? That's exactly why I try to avoid you sometimes."

Britney was shocked. She wanted to just disappear for a moment. But then a lightbulb went on. Keri was right. The two women started laughing together. "It looks like we both have something to work on," said Britney.

1. What do you feel is the primary message of the case on the previous page?

Its easier to see things in other people than in yourself -

2. Do you think Britney's observation was correct?

_____

_____

3. Do you think Keri's response was appropriate?

_____

_____

4. Is there a message in the case that you can personally relate to?

We all have things to work on

_____

The following page contains a feedback receptiveness quiz that relates directly to you.

FEEDBACK RECEPTIVENESS QUIZ

Answer the following questions as honestly as possible.

As a general rule:

Yes **No**

❑ ❑ **1.** I get embarrassed when people point out my mistakes.

❑ ❑ **2.** I resent people telling me what they think of my shortcomings.

❑ ❑ **3.** I regularly ask friends and associates I trust to comment on how I'm doing.

❑ ❑ **4.** I know how to offer constructive criticism to others in a sensitive way.

☑ ❑ **5.** I like people who tell me their reactions to my activities because it will help me adapt my future behavior.

If you answered a definite "yes" to items 1 and 2 you may be putting up some attitude barriers that could deter you from obtaining useful feedback. We are normally uncomfortable when we receive harsh or insensitive feedback, but even that can be valuable, if we take it in perspective. Even our worst critic can provide a "gift" of good advice, if we don't allow the emotion of the moment to blind us. Successful people learn how to develop an attitude of looking for a gem of good advice even when it's buried under a lot of worthless noise.

If you answered "yes" to items 3 and 4 you are creating a climate in which helpful feedback is accepted and expected. Organizations fostering such a climate are typically positive places to work and successful in their results. In a similar fashion, individuals who foster an attitude of being "receptive" receive the benefit of input from others.

If you answered "yes" to item 5, you are probably a little unusual. But you're on the right track.

The preceding material on assertiveness and receptiveness was adapted from Successful Self-Management, *by Paul R. Timm, Ph.D., Crisp Publications, 1993.*

Building a Network

Without realizing it, you have probably already built a network of professional colleagues who are willing to help and advise you. Your network consists of people both inside and outside of your organization who know you and your work. Key associates in your network keep you abreast of "what's happening." They may be in the same industry or field as you, or they may give you tips on developments in unrelated fields.

Why do you need a network?

➤ To give and receive support, advice, and insight

➤ To exchange specific information about trends, personnel changes, and career opportunities

➤ To transact business, or get a (perhaps new or unfamiliar) job done

Networking is a two-way street. When you invest time and energy in other people, they become valuable allies when you, in turn, need support or information. This is called a mutually rewarding relationship.

Are you setting up a conference? Putting out a newsletter? Reorganizing a department? Making a major office purchase? These are occasions when you can use your network. Why reinvent the wheel when you can consult others who have faced the same challenges?

Identify people who have contributed to your career:

➤ Who has been there to help you at an unexpected time?

➤ Who has encouraged you to change career directions and given good advice?

➤ Who has helped you develop your skills?

Giving back:

➤ Whom have you helped in their advancement?

➤ Whom have you shared contacts with?

➤ Whom are you willing to mentor?

HOW TO BUILD A NETWORK AND KEEP IT ALIVE

1. Always ask (and write down for future reference) the name of someone who has proven helpful with a project. Tell that person you would be glad to reciprocate, should the need arise.

2. If you meet someone whose work really impresses you, ask about his or her background, what training courses or materials have been useful, what reading he or she recommends, etc.

3. Send letters of praise or congratulations to people in your office or industry who receive honors or special recognition, maybe even to people you have never met.

4. A planned "open house" for your office can be a welcome surprise—and lead to warmer contact with other departments, suppliers, clients, outside sales representatives, etc.

5. If your organization encourages public-service involvement, volunteer—it's a great way to meet people you would not ordinarily see.

6. If you need (or desire) further training or education to meet your goals, find someone to advise and direct you.

7. Draw an organizational chart of your company. Promise yourself to develop at least one contact from every major part of it.

8. Join a trade or industry group appropriate to your organization.

9. Don't forget your personal network. Maybe you have friends or family members who could give you useful professional advice. Ask them.

Professional Organizations

You may be unaware of the professional organizations that promote better recognition on the job and certify skills. The International Association of Administrative Professionals (IAAP), formerly Professional Administrators International, has approximately 700 chapters and 40,000 members and affiliates worldwide. IAAP offers the Certified Professional Secretary® (CPS®) program, which involves a rigorous exam covering finance, business law, economics, office technology, office administration, business communications, behavioral science in business, human resources management, organizations, and management.

International Association of Administrative Professionals (IAAP)
10502 N.W. Ambassador Drive
Post Office Box 20404
Kansas City, MO 64195-0404
(816) 891-6600
www.iaap-hq.org

Other organizations that promote professional excellence:

American Business Women's Association
9100 Ward Parkway
Post Office Box 8728
Kansas City, MO 64114-0728
(816) 361-6621
(800) 228-0007
www.abwahq.org

Teaches leadership skills, encourages continuing education, provides workshops and seminars, awards over $3 million in scholarships annually. 60,000 members.

The National Federation of Business and Professional Women's Clubs, Inc.
2012 Massachusetts Avenue, N.W.
Washington, DC 20036
(202) 293-1100

Provides leadership training, career-related seminars. Offers networking opportunities. 73,000 members.

The National Association for Female Executives
135 West 50th Street, 16th Floor
New York, NY 10020
(212) 445-6235
(800) 634-NAFE
www.nafe.com

A major association dedicated to professional growth for female employees.

In Australia, contact:
The Institute of Professional Secretaries
Post Office Box 3167
Sydney, NSW 2001
www.ipsa.ca.com.au

Resolving Conflict in Your Office

Conflict is inevitable whether an office consists of two people or 10,000 people. However, with your attitude tuned to "positive," your value as a problem solver among people has unlimited potential.

Here are some standard sources of conflict in the workplace. For each category, write a brief example of conflict you have personally observed:

Sources of Conflict

An organization whose structure encourages conflict (perhaps by making workers compete against one another for special rewards)

Sales - Competition

Aggressive co-workers

Someone trying to advance to a higher position in the Company

Competition for resources (e.g., only one computer for three workers)

Use of a pooled laptop or LCD Projector

Power struggles (i.e. who will head the new department)

Handing over leadership of a group to new head person

Organizational change (people use many tricks to avoid changing comfortable routines)

Intergration of two Companies into one

Unresolved previous conflicts (even when the current issue should present no problems, previous grudges may interfere)

Non-trust of a colleague based on a previous conflict

Differences in facts and assumptions

Assuming it is OK to Change details of a meeting without consulting the person who is in charge

Customs and habits

Cultural differences regarding holidays and time off

Goals and expectations

Manager does not spend time in setting goals and expectations

Roles

Reporting to one person - supporting more than one person in a manager's role

Methods and styles

ONE person's method or style may not work with the way you feel comfortable in doing something.

RESOLVING CONFLICT
(SIX EASY STEPS)

Anticipating conflict (and knowing its causes, such as those you just listed) is one of the best ways to head off a situation before it erupts. When a conflict exists, either for you, or among other people in your organization, try using the following steps to maintain a positive environment.

1. **Schedule a meeting with the other party.**

   Decide on a time and place to sit down and discuss differences. That way you have each made a gesture toward resolution. Example: Debra, your department bookkeeper, resists your requests for statistics you need to include in regular reports. Think about the ideal time and place to meet with her, and say, "We need to talk about our working relationship and how it can be improved."

2. **Evaluate the cause.**

   First acknowledge that there is a conflict. (Not admitting there's a problem makes it worse.) Talk nonjudgmentally about the reasons for your differences.

3. **Use "I" messages.**

   Say "I thought you wanted this," or "I heard you say that." In this way, you avoid destructive accusations. Here is a pattern for an "I" message:

   I (feel, react)_____when you (act, do)_____which causes (consequences) _____.

4. **Encourage the other person to express his or her feelings.**

   Ask questions that draw out what the other person is thinking. Use phrases like "I would like your reaction to what happened," or "I would like to hear your reasons." In our example, the bookkeeper might say that she had no idea of the importance of the reports you worked on, or who needed the figures. She might also point out that you are often late giving her the information she needs for the report. The idea is to let the other party know that you are truly listening carefully to his or her opinions.

5. Structure your desired outcome.

Negotiate. Be sure that you each contribute to the "solution" and feel satisfied that it is at least worth trying. (Not every problem is going to be solved overnight, but progress can usually be made, even on those that are most difficult.) Some people like to write down agreements; but for most office situations, a handshake symbolizes mutual respect and agreement to work toward a solution.

6. Evaluate.

It's a good idea to set a definite time in the future (a week, a month, etc.) to evaluate the solution. When you successfully negotiate a conflict using the above guidelines, you will be amazed at how powerful you feel. Your power is not to push other people around, but to improve communications with those who may have different views.

CONFLICT RESOLUTION EXERCISE

Answer the following questions:

With whom do you have a conflict?

1. _____

2. _____

3. _____

4. _____

5. _____

What is the essence of this conflict?

_____

_____

_____

_____

_____

_____

_____

Choose one of your examples and complete the following questions:

1. How could you apply the six steps of conflict resolution for this conflict?

2. What happens if you choose not to express yourself?

You and Your Manager: A Unique Relationship

Normally you will not establish a special working relationship with your manager instantly. Like most other relationships, it will develop over time. The quality of the ultimate working relationship will be made up of countless small incidents that demonstrate to each of you what to expect from the other.

Your professional abilities are important. But even more significant is your desire to carry out your tasks in a way that "fits" with your manager's goals and style.

What Makes a Good Manager?

Administrators, coordinators, and secretaries who are most satisfied with their jobs describe a good manager as:

➤ A manager who shows respect and fairness toward all employees

➤ A person who builds mutual rapport and trust, and is willing to share ideas and goals

➤ One who has the qualities of a good teacher, such as clarity and patience when delegating new tasks

➤ A person who will delegate with trust, but who also monitors assignments and provides helpful feedback

➤ A boss who meets regularly with you (preferably daily) to set priorities and goals

➤ One who encourages everyone to seek improvements in office functions and procedures and listens when improvements are suggested

➤ An individual who is accessible on a regular basis, despite a frantic schedule or problems in certain departments (one who does not "blow up" in anger very often)

➤ A well-mannered person who says "thank you" and shows special appreciation for extra effort

Can you add other factors that identify a good manager? _____

Over time, you can influence your manager's behavior and attitude by modeling professional behavior. Remember: your attitude affects everyone around you—especially your manager.

CREATING A STATUS REPORT FOR YOUR MANAGER

Many employees have found that submitting a weekly or monthly status report is helpful in communicating problems. Although status reports take time, they are effective in keeping your manager informed and creating a record of what you've done, which can be helpful for performance evaluations or job interviews.

Sample Status Report

Name: Date:

Completed assignments:

a)

b)

c)

d)

Status on current projects:

a)

b)

c)

d)

Anticipated problems or concerns:

a)

b)

c)

d)

Adapted from Managing Upward, *by Patti Hathaway and Susan Schubert, Crisp Publications, 1992.*

TIPS FOR ESTABLISHING GOOD RAPPORT WITH YOUR MANAGER

1. Observe your manager's natural pace of work, and adjust your methods accordingly. Tension results when you do not understand priorities; try to figure these out as soon as possible.

2. Most managers need you to act as a buffer between them, email, the telephone, or unexpected visitors. Learn which people are welcome at any time, and which should be screened or helped by you.

3. Open channels of communication, especially about "little" things such as the preferred way of answering the phone, whether or not your manager always wants you to ask who is calling, whether he or she wants to let anyone else take material out of certain files, etc.

4. Realize that you often know more than your manager about certain incidents, procedures, and/or relationships in the workplace. Keep your manager informed about situations that are important.

5. "Save" your manager when he or she drafts a letter or memo in anger or misplaces an important paper. You might delay sending an angry letter for a day, and then have your manager read it for "errors." With the lost paper, think of ways it might have been incorrectly filed, and help with the search. (Keep a chronological file of every key paper coming in and going out: this has solved many crises.)

6. Stay within your authority. Do not use your manager's status as a way of pushing other people around. The more important your manager, of course, the greater your own power. But if you abuse it, it will reflect poorly on both of you. (Example: If your manager asks you to tell someone to turn in a report at their earliest convenience, don't say, "My boss wants this immediately.")

7. Help your manager keep to his or her schedule. Work out a method for you to interrupt long-winded visitors or telephone callers without offending anyone.

8. Above all, protect and preserve your manager's faith in your loyalty. Your manager's (and your) reputation can rest on your ability to keep information private and confidential.

Limiting Interruptions

Because you have the opportunity to interact with so many different people, you are likely to have many interruptions. It is appropriate to limit your interruptions when they interfere with your work. Because of the nature of your relationship with your manager, you may find that he or she is the greatest source of interruption although there will be many others including peers, vendors, contractors, and other managers. Here are some tips for limiting interruptions:

➤ Hold stand-up meetings. This eliminates unnecessary socializing. Do not sit down when you go into a co-worker's office.

➤ When a co-worker who visits often or takes up too much of your time comes into your office, stand up immediately.

➤ Be assertive and learn to say "no" with tact and diplomacy. When you do say "no," acknowledge the request, explain why you cannot accommodate it, and provide alternative solutions.

ASSESS YOUR RELATIONSHIP-BUILDING SKILLS

Rate the frequency with which you perform the following activities.

5 = always; 4 = most of the time; 3 = sometimes; 2 = rarely; 1 = never

_5_ Attend work-related conferences when available

_5_ Advise decision-makers of my interest in advancement

_5_ Participate in meetings or other group activities

_5_ Speak positively about my company to outside people

_5_ Attend seminars, courses, speeches to expand skills

_5_ Seek increased responsibilities such as serving on committees, project teams, etc.

_5_ Belong to at least one work-related organization such as a trade association

_5_ Go the extra mile to satisfy customers

_5_ Make changes or suggest ways to improve work

_5_ Maintain exemplary attendance records

_5_ Work on aspects of my performance that need improvement

_3_ If I have personal conflict, find ways to resolve it

Add up your responses and compare your score to the table below.

12 to 20: Very Low
Very low scores indicate you are not moving ahead. You may believe many of the career myths, including the one that people get ahead by just doing their work.

20 to 30: Low
Low scores suggest that you have developed career skills in some areas but not in others. Identify where you need to improve.

30 to 40: Medium
Medium scores imply that you are not overly fearful of reaching for success. Sharpen your career goals and continue to use self-promotion techniques.

40 to 50: High
High scores indicate self-confidence and ambition. You have excellent prognosis for success. You know what your goal is and how to reach it.

50 to 60: Very High
Very high scores suggest that you are probably already reaping career success.

Checklist for Success

Working toward professional excellence leads in many directions. The following checklist will help you analyze your job performance and set goals for the future growth.

When considering my job, I will:

❑ Identify how my job fits into the organization as a whole

❑ Describe the "service" my office provides

❑ Look for ways to do my job more effectively

To assess my professional goals and image, I will:

❑ Determine my career goals

❑ Begin changing my daily behaviors in order to achieve professional growth

In my role as office coordinator, I will:

❑ Survey my daily tasks and begin setting priorities

❑ Avoid procrastination and dependence on non-existent "catch up" time

❑ Determine several important long-range goals for my office and block out periods of time to work on them

❑ Practice making decisions by considering a variety of alternatives, rating them, and then taking action

❑ Set up a system to record work assignments and to get help when overloaded

❑ Learn about career-building classes in my area

❑ Write letters and memos only after considering (1) the audience, and (2) the simplest, quickest way to state the message

❑ Realize that every phone call can deliver quality customer service

❑ Plan impromptu speeches by breaking the subject matter into logical parts, and summarizing main points at the end

❑ Create checklists for planning, evaluating, and following up after meetings

To build good working relationships, I will:

❑ See office relationships as a chance to listen to and learn about a wide variety of other people

❑ Practice expressing my own opinions and decisions in a friendly, positive manner

❑ Build a network of helpful colleagues, both inside and outside my organization, who could contribute to my success

❑ Recognize that conflict occurs whenever people work together and practice discussing and resolving issues as they arise

❑ Arrange my work schedule to best meet my manager's needs, remaining flexible enough to accommodate unexpected changes

To complete my professional image, I will:

❑ Choose clothing and accessories that are appropriate for professionals in my office

❑ Be conscious of my non-verbal communications—i.e., posture, eye contact, personal habits—and keep them in tune with the rest of my image

❑ Assess the appearance of my work area and see it as an extension of my professional portrait

Professional Development

Answer the questions below as honestly as possible. They will help guide you to apply what you have learned from this book. Write brief responses in the space provided.

1. What are your personal career objectives?

   _____

   _____

2. What new skills have you learned recently that will help you achieve your goals?

   _____

   _____

3. What training have you taken to enhance your professionalism?

   _____

   _____

4. What training do you plan to take this year?

   _____

   _____

5. What professional literature have you read in the past few months?

   _____

   _____

6. What networks or organizations do you now belong to?

   _____

   _____

7. What are your plans for professional development in the next year?

   _____

   _____

8. How do you intend to apply what you have learned from this book to your leadership skills?

   _____

   _____

Personal Action Plan

The best intentions in the world lead nowhere unless they are put into action. By completing this book, you have said "yes" to career growth. The next step is putting your plans into writing and setting up a time schedule.

Using the Checklist for Success on the previous pages, select three "I Will" statements that would help you perform your job in a more professional manner. Then, after each statement, write how you will fulfill your goal, and one (or more) steps you could take tomorrow to begin.

Example: *I will set up a system to record work assignments and to get help when overloaded. Possible methods: I will purchase a notebook, setting up columns for the date, the assignments, their projected time requirements, and their due dates. Then I will discuss the usefulness of the notebook with my manager, and suggest ways of obtaining assistance when needed. What I can do tomorrow: Purchase the notebook, set up the columns, possibly have the discussion with my manager.*

Your Goals

1. I will:

_____

Method:

_____

_____

_____

Tomorrow I will:

_____

_____

_____

2. I will:

_____

When you regularly repeat this method of goal setting, you will feel your attitude improve and your energy increase. Keep this book handy and use it for recording your goals. Good luck.

Additional Reading

Johnson, Spencer. *Who Moved My Cheese?* New York: G.P. Putnam's Sons, 1998.

Manning, Marilyn and Patricia Haddock. *Leadership Skills for Women.* Menlo Park, CA: Crisp Publications, 1995.

Manning, Marilyn and Patricia Haddock. *Office Management: A Productivity and Effectiveness Guide.* Menlo Park, CA: Crisp Publications, 2001.

Oakley, Ed and Doug Krug. *Enlightened Leadership.* New York: Fireside, 1994.

Tannen, Deborah. *Talking from 9 to 5.* New York: William Morrow, 1994.

Tichy, Noel. *The Leadership Engine: How Winning Companies Build Leaders at Every Level.* New York: Harper Business, 1997.

Ury, William. *Getting Past No.* New York: Bantam Books, 1993.

Zemke, Ron and John Woods. *Best Practices in Customer Service.* New York: AMACOM, 1999.

NOTES

NOTES

NOTES

NOTES

VERK

CRISP WORLDWIDE DISTRIBUTION

English language books are distributed worldwide. Major international distributors include:

ASIA/PACIFIC

Australia/New Zealand: In Learning, PO Box 1051, Springwood QLD, Brisbane,
Australia 4127   Tel: 61-7-3-841-2286, Facsimile: 61-7-3-841-2618
ATTN: Messrs. Gordon

Philippines: National Book Store, Inc., Quad Alpha Centrum Bldg, 125 Pioneer Street,
Mandaluyong, Metro Manila, Philippines   Tel: 632-631-8051, Facsimile: 632-631-5016

Singapore, Malaysia, Brunei, Indonesia: Times Book Shops. Direct sales HQ:
STP Distributors, Pasir Panjang Distrientre, Block 1 #03-01A, Pasir Panjang Road.
Singapore 118480   Tel: 65-2767626, Facsimile: 65-2767119

Japan: Phoenix Associates Co., Ltd., Mizuho Bldng, 3-F, 2-12-2, Kami Osaki,
Shinagawa-Ku, Tokyo 141   Tel: 81-33-443-7231, Facsimile: 81-33-443-7640
ATTN: Mr. Peter Owans

CANADA

Crisp Learning Canada, 60 Briarwood Avenue, Mississauga, ON L5G 3N6 Canada
Tel: 905-274-5678, Facsimile: 905-278-2801
ATTN: Mr. Steve Connolly

Trade Book Stores: Raincoast Books, 8680 Cambie Street,
Vancouver, BC V6P 6M9 Canada
Tel: 604-323-7100, Facsimile: 604-323-2600   ATTN: Order Desk

EUROPEAN UNION

England: Flex Training, Ltd., 9-15 Hitchin Street,
Baldock, Hertfordshire, SG7 6A, England
Tel: 44-1-46-289-6000, Facsimile: 44-1-46-289-2417   ATTN: Mr. David Willetts

INDIA

Multi-Media HRD, Pvt., Ltd., National House,
Tulloch Road, Appolo Bunder, Bombay, India 400-039
Tel: 91-22-204-2281, Facsimile: 91-22-283-6478   ATTN: Messrs. Aggarwal

SOUTH AMERICA

Mexico: Grupo Editorial Iberoamerica, Nebraska 199, Col. Napoles, 03810 Mexico, D.F.
Tel: 525-523-0994, Facsimile: 525-543-1173   ATTN: Señor Nicholas Grepe

SOUTH AFRICA

Alternative Books, PO Box 1345, Ferndale 2160, South Africa
Tel: 27-11-792-7730, Facsimile: 27-11-792-7787   ATTN: Mr. Vernon de Haas